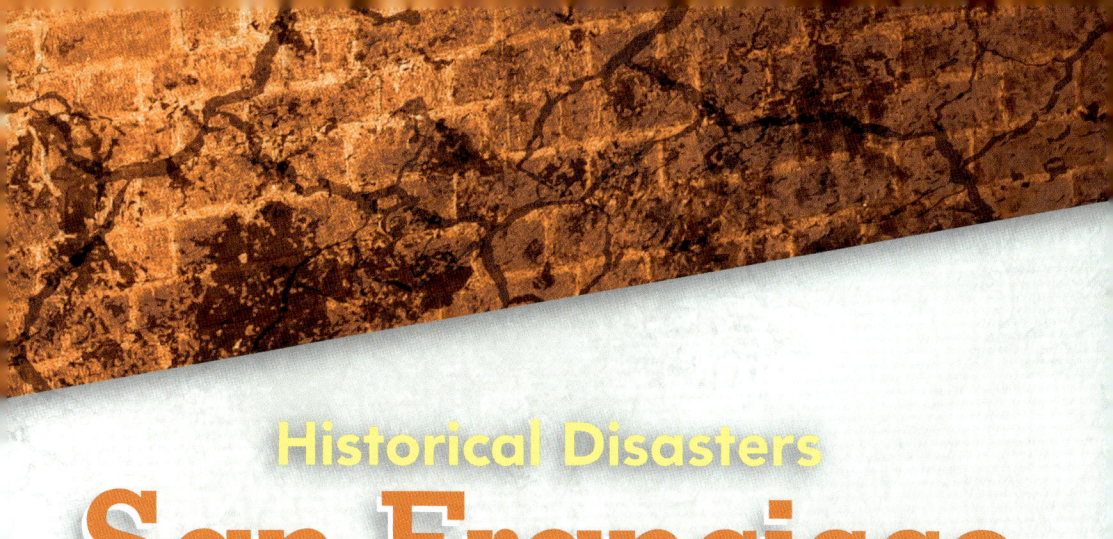

Historical Disasters
San Francisco Earthquake

by Julie Murray

Dash!
LEVELED READERS
An Imprint of Abdo Zoom • abdobooks.com

Level 1 – Beginning
Short and simple sentences with familiar words or patterns for children who are beginning to understand how letters and sounds go together.

Level 2 – Emerging
Longer words and sentences with more complex language patterns for readers who are practicing common words and letter sounds.

Level 3 – Transitional
More developed language and vocabulary for readers who are becoming more independent.

abdobooks.com

Published by Abdo Zoom, a division of ABDO, PO Box 398166, Minneapolis, Minnesota 55439. Copyright © 2024 by Abdo Consulting Group, Inc. International copyrights reserved in all countries. No part of this book may be reproduced in any form without written permission from the publisher. Dash!™ is a trademark and logo of Abdo Zoom.

Printed in the United States of America, North Mankato, Minnesota.
052023
092023

Photo Credits: Alamy, Getty Images, Shutterstock
Production Contributors: Kenny Abdo, Jennie Forsberg, Grace Hansen, John Hansen
Design Contributors: Candice Keimig, Neil Klinepier

Library of Congress Control Number: 2022947150

Publisher's Cataloging in Publication Data
Names: Murray, Julie, author.
Title: San Francisco earthquake / by Julie Murray
Description: Minneapolis, Minnesota : Abdo Zoom, 2024 | Series: Historical disasters | Includes online resources and index.
Identifiers: ISBN 9781098281250 (lib. bdg.) | ISBN 9781098281953 (ebook) | ISBN 9781098282301 (Read-to-me ebook)
Subjects: LCSH: Disasters--Juvenile literature. | History--Juvenile literature. | San Francisco Earthquake and Fire, Calif., 1906--Juvenile literature.
Classification: DDC 979.461--dc23

Table of Contents

San Francisco Earthquake 4

The Quake 8

The Aftermath 18

More Facts 22

Glossary 23

Index 24

Online Resources 24

San Francisco Earthquake

4

In 1906, San Francisco was the largest city on the West Coast. About 400,000 people lived there. It was a major business location that was rapidly growing.

San Francisco sits near the San Andreas Fault. This is where two of Earth's **plates** meet. On April 18, 1906, these plates collided. It caused a major earthquake in San Francisco and the surrounding areas.

The Quake

At 5:12 a.m. the ground in San Francisco began to shake. Most people were fast asleep. The 7.9 earthquake violently shook everyone out of bed. It lasted for almost 60 seconds!

While the earthquake's **epicenter** was located near San Francisco, it was felt many miles away. People in Oregon, Nevada, and southern California also felt the earthquake.

Many buildings in the city crumbled to the ground. City Hall was one of them. Water and gas lines burst open. The leaking gas **ignited** fires throughout the city.

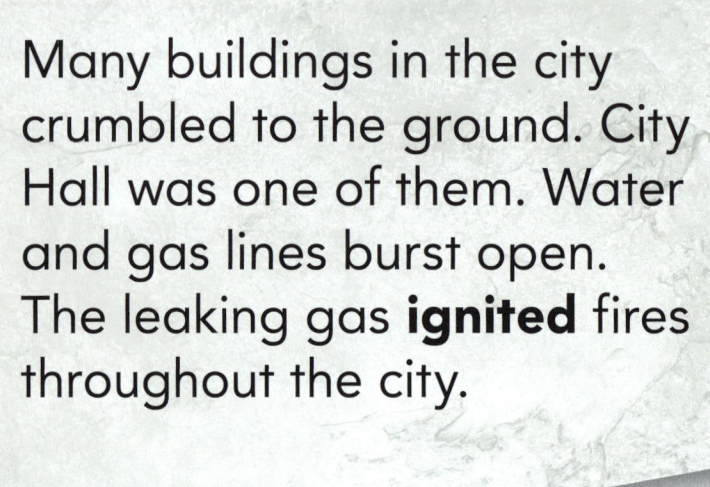

The fires burned for three days. Many structures were made of wood and built close together. This allowed the flames to jump from one building to the next.

More than 3,000 people lost their lives and 28,000 structures were burned. More than half of the city's population was left homeless.

The Aftermath

The city had to work hard to rebuild. Steel was used to reinforce buildings. People used fewer flammable materials in construction.

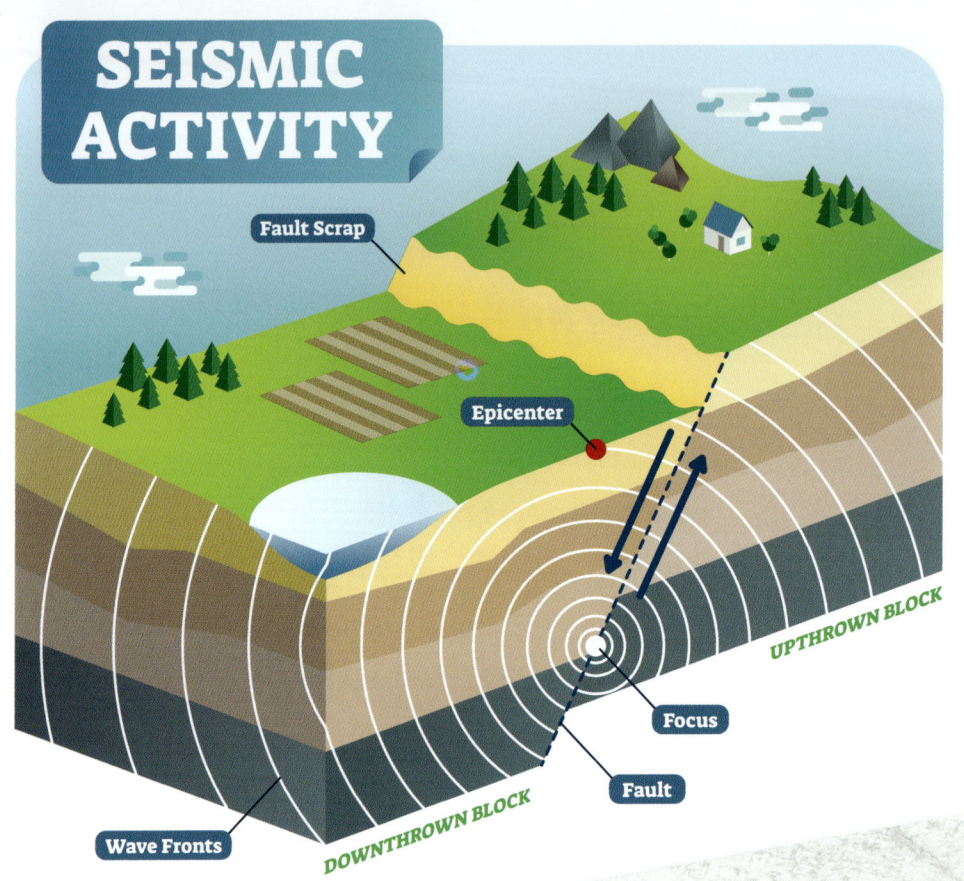

Scientists learned a lot from the earthquake. One discovery was that **friction** occurs along fault lines. As **plates** shift, energy stores up. Eventually, the energy releases and results in an earthquake.

More Facts

- A major **aftershock** occurred at 8:14 a.m. This caused more damage and chaos in the city. Aftershocks continued for months.

- The earthquake caused more than $400 million in damages. Today, that would equal about $13 billion!

- More than 500 city blocks were destroyed by the earthquake and resulting fires.

Glossary

aftershock – a small earthquake that follows a larger one.

epicenter – the point on the earth's surface directly above the central source of an earthquake.

friction – the resistance of a surface to motion.

ignited – caused to begin burning.

plate – a tectonic plate, one of the parts of the outer layer of planet Earth. The plates cover the whole planet. They move very, very slowly and touch each other as they move. Sometimes this contact can cause things like earthquakes and the building up of mountains.

Index

casualties 17

cause 6

damage 12, 15, 17

fires 12, 15

Nevada 10

northern California 5, 6, 9

Oregon 10

rebuilding 19

San Andreas Fault 6

Scientists 20

southern California 10

Online Resources

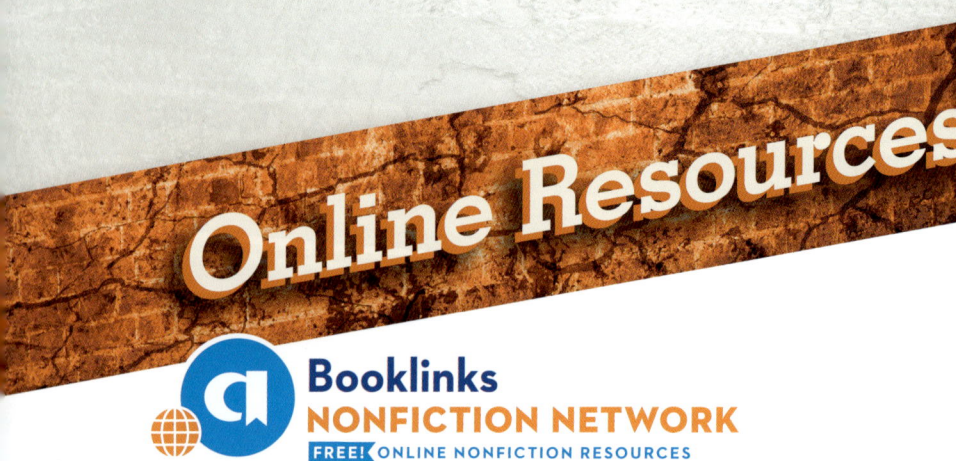

Booklinks
NONFICTION NETWORK
FREE! ONLINE NONFICTION RESOURCES

To learn more about the San Francisco earthquake, please visit **abdobooklinks.com** or scan this QR code. These links are routinely monitored and updated to provide the most current information available.